Who is Chak Mol?

By

Julia SvadiHatra

Who is Chak Mol?

iUniverse books may be ordered through booksellers or by contacting:

iUniverse
1663 Liberty Drive
Bloomington, IN 47403
www.iuniverse.com
1-800-Authors (1-800-288-4677)

Because of the dynamic nature of the Internet, any Web addresses or links contained in this book may have changed since publication and may no longer be valid. The views expressed in this work are solely those of the author and do not necessarily reflect the views of the publisher, and the publisher hereby disclaims any responsibility for them.

ISBN: 978-1-4401-4112-6 (pbk)
ISBN: 978-1-4401-4113-3 (ebk)

Printed in the United States of America

Editor: Roxane Christ www.1steditor.biz

Cover design: Most4u.net

iUniverse rev. date: 7/1/2009

Dedication

Dedicated to the creativity of the people who lived on Earth or will be living in the future.

Leonardo Da Vinci, Wolfgang Amadeus Mozart, Alexander Pushkin, Johann Sebastian Bach, Tchaikovsky, Lev Tolstoy, *Michelangelo, Rembrandt van Rijn*, George Friedrich Händel, Alfons Ven, "Abba", Elvis Presley, Rimsky Korsakov, *Albert Einstein*, "Enigma", *Galileo Galilee, Nicolaus Copernicus*, Nostradamus, Tesla, Mendeleyev, Marie Curie, Louis Pasteur, Stephen Hawking, *Jan Van Hyusum, Jan Davidsz de Heem, Edvard Grieg,* Peter Breughel, Pierre-Auguste Renoir, Frans Snyders, William Shakespeare, conductor Igor Golovchin, acter Jack Nicholson, opera singer Vecheclav Osipov, father of wave genetic P. Gariaev, child prodigy Akiane Kramarik, Connie Talbot ... *you can add any creative person you know...*

List of Dreams

1. *DESTRUCTION OF THE CRYSTAL SPHERE, February. 19, 1992*

2. *ELEVATORS WERE RINGING BECAUSE OF ME, September 12, 1992*

3. *ZARATUSTRA IN WATER, September 6, 1993*

Who is Chak Mol?

This intriguing question "Who is Chak Mol?" was one of the reasons for which I started writing this whole book.

Currently, the entire book includes 8 Chapters.
However, I decided to make these three short books as a gift, mainly for the Mexican people. Just to tell them about their history: about the real life of the Ancient Maya people in Chichen Itza and the life of their Priest 2000 years ago. Also, in the third book, I wanted to tell them: Who Chak Mol really was. Who is this popular hero? The name of whom I saw everywhere in Mexican villages. Sometimes it's the name for a coffee shop, or a store or a hair salon even. Who is Kukulcan?

I wish for these three books to be translated into Spanish, so it can be available to each and everyone in Mexico for a very small, affordable price.

I think it will be also interesting for the tourists in Chichen Itza, as well as for the scientists and especially for the archeologists who study Chichen Itza.

During one of the hypnosis readings about the Priest, I saw suddenly that the Maya people were talking to a huge, giant man!

It was a big shock for me and I just didn't know what to think!

The hypnosis readings' process was really new to me, and when I saw, for example, big, round, white earrings on the man's ears, I was sure this was my imagination.

Who is Chak Mol?

The same thing happened when I thought about this enormous, huge man that I saw during the reading. But when I traveled to Chichen Itza, after the first readings regarding the Priest, suddenly, to my big surprise, I saw men wearing these white, big, round button-earrings everywhere on the walls of the sites, and I decided to go again to Di Cherry to find out who this giant man among the Maya people was.

I asked Di Cherry during the reading to pay attention to what the small Maya people were doing, how they lived, and I told her that maybe I would see the giant again among them. As soon as the reading started I saw him again! Well, he was way too big not to see him!

Here is a short version of the reading. The full reading is available on CD which can be purchased at www.ameliareborn.com.

Reading; February 20, 2008

(Note: This reading, same as the others, is a literal transcription of the taped session – no editing.)

What do you feel, experience right now – tell me?

I think I saw this big man again, it's near the entrance! But he can not go in, he so big, he staying near entrance. His eyes blue and his hair white.

Tell me what they call that man?
Can you hear his name been used?

See I know that they say Chak Mol. So this ...it kind of come another name....it is Paw...

But I see his legs, his feet very big, I see them now, it is very big feet

And if you look at him you look up like to the mount...far... he is big

And his voice? Is it gentle or like a thunder?
When he speaks to you how he speaks to you?
Tell me about his voice.

He is so big and strong and scary – his voice, cause it's so loud. It's like a Thunder, yes.

Yea... he needs to lie down to talk, because when he sits he's also too high.
He could not see your expression if he's way up there.

You said before that he looks more like a European man than a Mayan.
Can you tell me more about him?

He has very light eyes, very light blue eyes.

Blue?

Yes, blue eyes and his hair up to shoulder. He has tone also, but I have darker tone, much darker than him.

But you're not the same race that he is?

No.

Tell me, could you ask him if he was born here somewhere in this area?

(Suddenly my voice changes dramatically, it starts sounding like many voices speaking at once, talking at the same time, with an echo....)

(Note: You should hear it! I am amazed when I hear it myself! It sounds like the voice I had during my first

7

reading. But we did not record it. This sound feels as if it came through a time-tunnel between the past and future, through the great distance separating us from thousands of years back, and affected by TIME'S vibration; one voice split into many voices with an echo.)

No, he's born far away, he was born far away.

Okay. Across the water?

Yes, he was born across the water. He was born in BIG pyramid, in big pyramid, pyramid. Turquoise color shiny big pyramid.

And..., and the other people with him were as tall as he is?

Like his mother, yes. His mother has gold hair, very tall... I saw her now, beautiful. This is his mother.

When you see his mother, is she giving birth or she holding him or is she talking to him? What are you experiencing?
(Pause....)
Do you know if you've been in this country, this country from where he comes from? Did you ever live in this country, too?
At first when you start talking, when I talk about his mother... you start asking me. I was sure that I am his mother...
(Start crying)

I am his mother as well. I was his mother.[1]

---

[1] According to many psychics before we are born, we establish some kind of program for the next life. The program contains goals that will assist us in the development of our Soul and Spirit, as much as possible. We sign a contract with some High Spiritual Authorities on the "Other side". We choose gender,

I see.... No wonder, if he can live up to 800 years old, I see how it's possible.
So, tell me about this pyramid. Tell me are you inside of this pyramid? Outside of it? Are you walking on the steps of the pyramid?

I think it very big sphere, it huge sphere, maybe kind of 1/3 of the round big huge sphere, it like biggest hall.

This is big hall, hall as a big space, very big space, huge space.

Right.

And they have big crystal inside, very big huge crystal inside.

Is this crystal clear crystal or colored?

Maybe it is just little bit turquoise or it is reflection. And I know how operate this crystal, I know.

---

parents, family, country, set of qualities, and the time and place of our birth, which will help in the realization of the contract. The person does not remember this contract when he or she is born, but if the person lives the right way he or she will be lucky, lead a happy life and feel the support from the High Power. I read that, in India, people often reincarnate and are reborn in the same family or in the same village or community.

It looks like Chak Mol's mother, a woman from Atlantis, chose to be born as a Priest to be close to her son, for them to be together, and to work with him, to help him and to complete her own program at the same time. After Atlantis sank, Egypt and Mexico, I guess were the only two nations with the highest-level of culture development on Earth – maybe China as well.

9

Who is Chak Mol?

Good, is that your job? Is that things that you do? Do you pray to operate the crystal or put your hands to the special way?

In my dream it was like a galaxy, round things...you doing with your hand and after it starts like a strong sound, terrible sound, like a very, very strong thunder kind sound and this sound at same time like electricity like blow up...lots of blue things flying...huge things ....

It is very serious, it is not job and it's not responsibility. It is a necessity. It is necessary...to operate this crystal. Once, we have problem with small pyramid and I will need to fix it, so I have device in my hand and I work with big crystal and it some very strong power together create lighting and this electricity blow up effect and sound, strongest sound, but it may work out and I fix the problem.
But my palace... this sphere goes down on the top, start kind of flat on the top...and people worry...so worried... but it is okay. This one, it is okay, it is not important, we can fix it later. Most important, I did my job and we have another seven, and we have big one.

This knowledge very powerful and very dangerous to know for everybody and it's a big responsibility to operate with this, because it can destroy so much if operated the wrong way.

And does this crystal bring water? The rain?

(My voice changes again, it sounds as if there are many voices speaking at once, with an echo....)

I think I know ...I know now why they call him Thunder Paw. Because he remembers this knowledge from his mother, and I think he can create rain. He can create rain and when he doing this, this is what will be...it will be

10

this horrible sound, you know...horrible sound, which he makes with space and energy and crystal.

When you were in Atlantis and the mother of this man with the voice of Thunder, you must be nearly 12 feet tall then, is that right?

Yes. And near me another two also very tall, another two women. Very, very white everything beautiful and white around them and they wearing something really white . . . and two of them coming outside and its big stairs and very, very big white temple and white pillars. We are going outside and outside near the pillars many people staying, all kinds of clothes they have.... Another few crystals, big huge pyramids not far away from this place, you can see they all around.... One have round shape like sphere shape and exist another 7 like this and one biggest much bigger then all this one...and everybody look to the water and something with water, something under water....which bother everybody and we looking at this. We are kind of worried, not really worried...but kind of worry what is this and what is going on....we expecting of some big amount of somebody come out and it kind of danger...

****

Dream # 1
Destruction of the Crystal Sphere, February 19, 1992

I had not slept all night. I dosed for 5 minutes around 8:00 a.m. My electronic clock was still working, when I fell asleep, and when I woke up, it had stopped, although it worked during the night.[2] I think this was because of my dream.

I don't remember my entire dream. I was in a big building with a huge, endless hall. At the beginning, I was standing above this area, in the other premises of the building. Some girl approached me. She started saying something, something very important. It was not a warning about danger, it was some problem. I let her know that I would do it, and went on doing what I was supposed to do. I ran over "it" with my hand, or with my mind, but it was very important. It looked like a spiral Galaxy. I started making similar, circular movements with my right hand.[3] It was very much like another time, when I was sleeping once in 1988, and I woke up and saw how something (a Galaxy), a condensed energy, was buzzing with deep sound high over my bed, it was blue in color and it flashed.

I said to that girl – "I can do this, much stronger than it can be imagined". And I ran over it with my hand and it started buzzing, and after that, it started buzzing with a high frequency sound, like when you run with your finger around the rim of a wine glass. The sound became so hard, as if it was about to pierce your eardrums. In this "galaxy" – in this space – there were sparks of bright white color, like sparks from the trolleybus wires, with a tint of electric blue. Such sparks dropped down like snowflakes, or firework sparks. And this thing, itself – this kind of galaxy – was blinking. The thing consisted of sparks and the buzzing

---

[2]   Electric clocks, watches stopped. It was the same, as it happened before, after this kind of dream.

[3]   This very unusual movement of the hand repeated itself in many places, in many dreams and I even drew how the hand moved. In this dream, the movement of the hand connects with materialization, (see the *Atlantean abilities*).

sound went up and down, unbearable. The lighting was like a flashing light – and when it flashed, it turned into colors of light – electric purple, then red, then electric green.... Such colors are usually called acid colors. And the sparks were falling out of it. And when it was flashing, there were flashes of purple, lilac colors. It was beautiful. But then it was not about beauty, it was monstrous.

The "Galaxy" was to the left of me. On the right, at about a half a meter, there was a wall. But this thing was moving through it – as if there was no wall at all. You could see it, and everything around was unimportant.

Then there was a cracking sound, higher and higher, electric, clear, and it stopped.

I went out, got downstairs, there is a huge hall. There was a sphere in this hall – not hemisphere, but 1/3 of a sphere, it was in the middle, rising from the walls, up, as high as the skyscrapers of Vancouver. It was a crystal, and it consisted of some sort of thin hollow glass tubes, connected together like in a beehive, quite thin. Under the sphere there were people walking, the sphere was for them a kind of a roof – same as the conservatory in Queen Elizabeth Park in Vancouver. The sphere was of a very elaborate design, there were many strange pieces, and they were hanging down. For example, as if the *Zurvan tracings* were hanging down. Different forms, colors, long and short.

Anyway, when I was in that room upstairs, I was amazed, that I could do even more, than I assumed. When I was going down the white stairs into the hall, I saw a group of people, about 7 to 10 people. In the middle, or on the side, there is nothing there, no furniture, only a smooth, mirror-like floor. And I saw,

13

that because I did that thing upstairs, the sphere started to fall down, soften on one side. It cannot collapse, it is indivisible, and it started to move down – because of what I had done. And they all were looking at it, agitated, talking among themselves. But I didn't move a muscle. I did not feel myself a destructor. I remembered, what was supposed to happen. Everything was in order now. I had a feeling that I am a queen, and this sphere did not matter much to me. I knew much higher values. Let's assume that there were another seven of such spheres, and one more, a huge one – the main, the largest pyramid. What I had done was necessary. I had the feeling that I knew, but forgot about my capacities, but then I began to remember. I had a feeling that an important task had been fulfilled. Calm indifference.

Ancient Spiral Galaxy

Now I know how to control myself and the energy in these kinds of dreams, but years ago, I didn't. Usually, elevator, or phones are out of order and often, fire alarms start ringing in cases like these, and the fire trucks arrive right after that. My friend even wrote a song for his band, which is popular now, about a fire truck coming and "nothing to do here for us now."

I don't like shopping, because some days the electric buzzer near the entrance door of the store will start making this ringing sound. Even if I walk outside on Robson Street, where the stores are all in a row, one after another, the moment I pass near the open doors, this buzzer is activated and the sound follows me from one store to the next. The last time it happened, it had a stronger effect. It happened twice in the spring of 2004 in a period of two weeks, when I saw the same kind of dreams where I was experimenting with electricity and crystals. At first, the fire alarm went on in the whole of this nine-storey building. I felt guilty when the people ended up on the street at 3:30 a.m. with little sleepy kids in their arms or holding cages with cats and dogs. We had to stay there and wait for the fire trucks to arrive to check the building. There was no electricity in our block until the afternoon of that day. The next time, it was much more serious. My friend, Marina – a psychic – called me from New York in the morning and told me that she saw a powerful electrical station blow up in her dream, which was connected with me. She asked if I was okay. I was..., but from the moment I woke up from this dream, until the middle of the following night there was no electricity for the entire day in 5-7 blocks and all the stores on Davie Street, up to Burrard, were closed on that day.

Who is Chak Mol?

The elevator and car incident

Since Julia's limo driver mixed the day when he was to meet her when she returned from Europe, she called me and I met her at the airport. I did not see her for a long time. So, on the way back to town, I started sharing my problems with the manager of the building, where I live. I was extremely angry at him. Because of him, my locker room was opened a few times and lots of valuable stuff was stolen. I talked about it all the way into town. Julia warned me that she just had a dream about crystal pyramids in Atlantis and asked me to stop being angry, because she didn't want to be involved with my angry talk. She said she was very tired after a long flight and maybe it would be difficult for her to control her "electrical energy." I was sure she was kidding and didn't pay attention to what she said. I continued to express my anger. What happened next was unbelievable; the alternator and an axel in the car broke down as we arrived! Lucky it did not happen on the way.... It was silly for me to spend so much energy trying to remember bad things.... I got a good lesson. However, it Looked like my negative energy influence was still around Julia, it continued to have an electrical effect on things, because when we arrived with her suitcases in front of the elevator at her home (and I needed to return to my building), the elevators stopped working! I am lucky I was not inside! I walked down the 19 flights of stairs. Yes, her peaceful nature was disturbed by my negativity. You need to be positive when you are with her, you will be happier and maybe you will be blessed. If you are negative or rude it could mean punishment for you in some little or bigger ways, such as it happened with my car.

William, Julia's neighbor
June 6, 2008

Julia's body sometime produces very unusual, powerful electricity. It can affect phones, elevators, cars, fire alarms and so on. One astrologer found it in her chart. It says that sometimes it is dangerous for her to be in an aircraft, because it could affect its power distribution. It is good that she now knows and has began to control it. A long time ago, she didn't. Once she had some reason to be upset about something and she looked out the window of her place. Across the street, there was a row of steel garages, and near it, stood an old, little wooden shed. I remember the fire started suddenly and fire trucks arrived almost immediately. At first, I thought it was a false alarm as usual – fire trucks came from time to time because of her – but this time it was a real fire. It happened a few times during those years, because of this incredible energy emanating from her eyes, which ignited the things on which she focused when she was upset... However, and since she has controlled herself, it has not happened for many years. Nevertheless, the last time it happened, on the way to the train station was a stressful situation. She went to a bookstore to buy some rare book. People delayed her in the store and there was not much time left until the train was scheduled to leave. When she finally came out of the store, I dropped her and her daughter at the train station, and on the way home, the axel and alternator of my car broke down! I called the service to tow the car and bring it to the mechanics. I was sure Julia was responsible for this incident, because my car was in a perfect working condition when I left home to pick her up.

By the way, just a week earlier, my brother, Alex's car broke down for exactly the same reason. I had seen Julia pass near the car a few times calling her daughter to come home. She was playing with her cousin nearby that day and she had not come home for dinner on time. When Alex got to his car later, it was not working!

Who is Chak Mol?

Sometimes this sort of "electricity ability" of hers is helping her and people – she is one powerful lady.

Tim, August 30, 2008

Well, Tim still did not know that a couple of months earlier the alternator and axel broke down in William's car, after he picked me up at the airport. I didn't expect that this would happen or even twice in a two-month interval! I deeply wish to apologize to all three people....

Tim's car being towed away

****

We live in Belgium and in the Netherlands, and once we mentioned about Julia's abilities to our friend, who is psychic. When she started thinking about Julia, suddenly the electricity at her place began acting up. Her TV-set was turned on, and even after she pulled the plug out, it was still switched on! This scared her and she waited a week before she dared tell us about it. We then told her that Julia lived across the ocean in Canada. When we told Julia about this, she explained it as, "Easy. When we have day here in Europe, in Canada it's nighttime." During her night-dream, her Spirit may have felt this psychic attention and maybe electricity in the house started reacting to Julia's Spirit presence.

A few weeks later, Julia was coming to visit my nephew and his wife in Australia. I sent him a note (as a joke) saying, "A storm is coming," because my memory was fresh of our experiences with our psychic friend. They live on the top of a huge old volcano crater, below which there is a large valley. During the first night when Julia slept in the house, strange electricity problems occurred in town, they blew up the station in two places and there was no electricity from 11 PM until the next day (in a town of 75,000 people). That night, on the first of January 2009, Julia saw some global flooding in her dream; with waves two-third the height of the snow-capped mountains. That huge ocean wave inundated this valley and she tried to do something about it. I guess she saw fragments of her past life and flooding in Atlantis. The next evening an enormous storm and rain started, which beat all Australian records with a huge amount of lightning. There were some 80,000 lightning strikes recorded that night! The entire valley was under constant, bright, electricity light.

These three cases are, by some coincidence, connected with Julia, and all related to her presence in each area. There is already a list of the cases and witnesses, and it forms a pattern of occurrences. It looks like her ability from her past life as a queen in Atlantis is still a strong part of her Spirit even now.
Wim, *http://www.akaija.com/*

I try my best to control myself in my dreams. Since 2004 it never happened again, except in these three instances and I am really glad! It was very disturbing for me, so I even had a dream about it. This second dream occurred 8 months later, during the same year when I had most of the dreams about sphere palaces and working with pyramid energy.

Dream # 2
Elevators Were Ringing Because Of Me, September 12, 1992

I was walking down the street, it was getting dark. A man and a woman were walking arm in arm. She said to him, "I will invite 7 women to put my flat in order." They had already passed me; I ran after them and said, "Take me, right now." The man left and she turned back to her house. She said, "OK, but why do you want it?"

I said, "I have everything, I don't care about anything." Something like – I want to turn off my life, to have a respite from myself, to take care of somebody else's problems.

We entered a hotel. A doorman was near the door behind the front desk. I managed to pass somehow. Then we approached the big elevators. I said, "They torment me, always watch me. Everywhere, wherever I go, there is some kind of electricity, which reacts to me. They can trace me easily – in elevators, entrance doors, in a subway, shops, etc. They always know where I am, this secretive team of people. I am always asked, stopped in the most inappropriate places, they lead me there; maybe they are attuned to my moods in order to recognize me. They cannot kill me; they don't want to shake me or torment me. They even cannot interrogate me seriously. Everything is done in a friendly tone.

20

They cannot overdo it, maybe because they don't want my mechanism to be broken."

In this instance, when I wanted I went and visited "the others" – not people – but this secretive team of people, some wanted to know everything about the others. When I came to them, they asked me who the others were, what kind of weapons they had. I could transcend to the other world in a moment, by my own wish, like going one-step up. I had just one impression – our world was unpleasant, gray, and empty – the Stone Age – compared to another more dimensional one. There were others – very different from where we were here, very light, just like angels. It seemed strange to me, that the ones here were hostile to the others and sneaking about to learn about them. They didn't need to know about "the others". They could not even imagine – just a little bit – grasping the reverberation, the reflection in the mirror of those kinds of angels. But they would not mind trying to eliminate them. They were just like thickheaded ants, who wanted to clutch, to *press* down and to destroy.

There was a trick. When many people entered the elevator, it started ringing because it was overloaded, but it also rang because of me. I knew exactly how many people would create the ringing. So I waited with this woman, then we entered the elevator again, but the ringing continued – I had caused it and it was mixed with the passenger overload. One of the men left the elevator and we went up. We entered her flat. It was semicircular. At the window, which was supposed to look over the street, I saw the window of the other flat through it. It was like an anthill. I saw how the light went on in that other room, how the woman entered. I said, "Close the curtains, they will see us!" (I was afraid of being chased, somehow). Maybe it was the reason why I went to strangers, just not to be watched and

21

have a little rest from it. And here – a glass looking into the other glass! But that woman seemed not to see us. My woman told me, "Calm down. They don't see you. You see them but they don't."

Her furniture was very strange – small – up to your knees. The ceiling was just head-high. Everything in the room was up to your knees. I sat down – with difficulty – everything was so low. The wall was transparent from bottom to ceiling. It felt as if I was about 3 or 4 meters tall.[4]

Reading; March 25, 2008

(Note: This reading, same as the others, is a literal transcription of the taped session – no editing.)

I see again this big man, and I am on the left side on top and he's on the right side. Big men sitting again and he has feathers in his hair, he looks straight, he sits and he has outfit like all these people around . . . he looks with the same outfit . . . but . . . but he is different.

And he is inside this temple room with you?

No, no, no, he can not... His feet, he so big, he very big.

Okay.

He sit right now in front of pyramid from right side and the back, little bit at the back and he also waiting...and he have kind of little skirt and he have big bracelet on his

---

4   It looks like I was an Atlantean in this dream – very tall. This woman in the dream saw me but other people didn't or I just followed her. I wonder how I even fit in the apartment. I guess I touched the ceiling with my head. Number 7 again, it is the number of pyramids that were in Atlantis.

legs and in the hands. And yes, today he have hat, kind of hat, protection from sunshine. They make for him kind of sharp on the top, triangle kind of hat.
(Pause...)
And I see his face very good right now I see his face. He has blue eyes and he has dark skin, skin tone skin. And he has long this chin, long, long. And yes, he have nose little bit up on the end, it's like up on the end and its bump, I see this bump. And he has wrinkles near the eyes and he try to close his eyes from this sunshine. Killing sunshine, very hot...

So he squints. As I understand it, Thunder Paw can activate clouds, he can activate the clouds, and he can cause the rain. What else does his need?

We need to have clouds to have rain...you know, we need clouds to have rain. (Voice change)

Can Thunder Paw bring you clouds?

Thunder Paw he have bag, I see this bag. People make for him bag, same like a blankets, this Mexican blankets type of bag and he have crystal inside, I see this crystal inside. Its big crystal and it flat at the down, at the bottom, but it crystal and he have some kind of metal, I don't know, what this...something little something, things, like a... I can draw how it looks like, it like a device or something to active this crystal...I don't know the kind of he work with this crystal with this things he have ...

And, yes, and?

He very big... Thunder Paw very big...
When you stand beside Thunder Paw could he put his hand on your head?
(Worry voice...really worry)

Who is Chak Mol?

His hand so big and heavy! So big... heavy...

What he can do to you?

We friends with him, we are good friends...and when I talk with him...
He lies down... he lies down.
I walk to him now...I walk to him now...and he sit and I look at him up and even when he sit he too high and now he lie down to his elbow and I see his face so close now, right in front of me kind of. And he looks at me and he talk with me and he turns his head toward me now and he can talk with me...
Supposing now you looking at his face.

Is he wearing something behind his ears today?
Is he wearing a decoration?
Is it feathers?

He has hat...it's hot and his hat near him now on the land.
And this hat ...this hat very kind of complicated looks, it just hat on top, and on the top its same and it kind of strange... BUT he has, he has same like we have when we listen music now! These things he has and it's really big, it's really big and it's bigger then we have head phones. And it's like a head phone, like this shape but its big and thick, and it like button on the top. And it closes his ears when he wearing this...
I see it, and it's near him, he don't wearing this all the time, but just when it necessary...

Yes...

His name Thunder Paw, Thunder Paw.
When he starts talk it's so strong and loud, so I step back, because it so crazy loud when he talking.

24

He asks me talk with him very loud also. He did not hear too good... he did not hear too good. I need to scream to talk with him. I need to try talk loud with him.

And since you are so close to Thunder Paw, tell me does he have blue eyes?

Yes, you don't even ask I already feel that you will ask about blue eyes.
Because I look right to his eyes now and its blue turquoise eyes, blue eyes.

Turquoise blue?

Blue, blue eyes. Yes.

If I will look in your eyes, you must see your eyes.

I have dark deep blue eyes...he has light eyes.

I understand.

Like a rock, you can see, like a sapphire, like something very light...beautiful!
I have dark deep blue eyes.

Yes, I have seen these dark, deep blue eyes.

(Pause. Suddenly I start crying...)

His eyes he has same like his mother has. His mother has blue eyes...same eyes.

You knew his mother?

Yea, it's beautiful mother, he have beautiful mother...
(I continue crying)

Who is Chak Mol?

Big mother, she so tall this woman, so tall and slim and very, very tall mother and he loved his mother. He misses his mother....very much he miss mother...and he cry about his mother... he miss his mother... his mother so fare, so far away. He will never see his mother again...she so far away.

Does Thunder paw ever tell you about his father? You ever speak of his father?

I see his father, his father have curly blond, dark blond hair. I see his father. His father have nose like him, with little bump...and up at the end. His father have same nose.

Okay.

Yes and his father and his mother they king and queen of beautiful kingdom, beautiful kingdom, they live in beautiful white palace, big palace...

I see...

It's this side, right side from Mexico, right side. It's an island and it is a big island.
And they have big city, they big city there from the West side and city name...city name... Ollan..., Ollap..., Something...
This Kingdom... they have many big palace, but they looks like a sphere, they 1/3 of sphere... they not like a palaces we know, they sphere's palaces
And so many crystals, big crystals and statues and some crystals soooo big!!!

Perhaps it was once a part of Atlantis.

Yea...

At one time there was a big land here and I think it's an island now.

We need to ask you some questions about Chak Mol – or Chaak Mol.

Chal Mol is a Thunder Paw!

He comes from the same country?

It's the same person! Chak Mol is a Thunder Paw.

Right.

When he uses this crystal, when he uses this crystal he makes thunder, he makes real thunder!
It was lightning it was crazy strong lighting and it's very big loud sound, very big sound. And when he using this, he has his hat.

I see... This hat helps him hear things....

No.

No?

No, his hat ...he closed his ears.

Okay.

I guess he never uses before this hat and he starts losing his hearing, so now he protected his ears.

When you see pictures of him as a Chak Mol and see him lie down.
It's the famous carving of him where he lies down on his back.....

Who is Chak Mol?

Yes... (Start crying)
I feel him like my close friend. my close dear friend...I had so much time with him, we spend so much time with him...and I now I want just hug this statue.... this is my friend.

What he has got in his hand? Did he have a crystal when they made the carving of him? Was this a golden disk?

He has disk, very sharp slim disk, made from some strange metal, it's very thick and its very sharp like things, but it heavy...yes
It is very strong too
Yes, very powerful things he has...
It's rigid, it's strong. Yea.

And flexible.

Yes.
He also have big bowl to eat and everybody always bring something and give him and try feed him...cause he so big, he need to eat a lot....people love him...people love him...

What does he eat? Fruit?

Everything, beans, fruits...

Meat?

Yea. Sometimes...
He likes to play, he likes to run, he likes running.

And playing ball? Did you watch him play ball?

He have in his bag ball, yes, he have rubber ball in his bag, he have.

Is this ball too big for you, too heavy for you?

Yes, it's big ball and...

And? And now?

They build a wall and they put on top for him ring. And he play with this and he play, he play same when I was in school and it was fashion between children to play with fuzzy things, but heavy with their legs and with legs and they kick with legs and with knee ...and he play same way...

So we need to come back to this day, when you're waiting for rain, you're waiting for a cloud. All the people who came here are waiting to hear you speak, waiting for you to do something, so they can have rain and plant their crops.

YES...
This is another day, this is another day...

Then tell me about another day.

This day was later... it was when Chak Mol left, he left us and he not near anymore...and he can not help me, he can not help us... he left ...we have drought ... we have... and people need water, people can give anything for this water. And this day so important, it's very important. We pray God to help us.
And when Chak Mol left, when he left, this Thunder Paw...we make statue of him. I miss him...and in my kind of office with jaguar, near jaguar we put his statue... I ask...case I miss him ...I want him near...

****

29

Who is Chak Mol?

I had numerous hypnosis sessions. Di Cherry told me that after each session during the next 2 or 3 weeks, I would be in this special state of mind where I would continue to see more and more. It was a real shock for me during the first reading when I saw for the first time this huge giant, a real live man, sitting near his platform between small Maya people!

Literally, I just couldn't believe my eyes! It was impossible to understand who this man was. Why was he so big and how could he possibly exist, because he was such a real huge human!

On top of this, I did not see it as we see things at the movie theater, for example. I was suddenly right near him! And when, during the reading, Di Cherry asked: "What will happen if he puts his hand on your head?"

"I was scared!" My voice dropped... "I was worried because his hand was too big and heavy!"

A month ago, I was in Acumal, Mexico on the Maya Riviera. I visited the Yal Ku Park there. This park is amazing! It is filled with beautiful statues made by different artists. Some of the statues are located on a small island surrounded by the ocean lagoon. There, I saw a very unusual kind of statue made by the same artist - CHARLOTTE YAZBEC.

Yal Ku Park
(Statue by CHARLOTTE YAZBEC)

I think this woman, in her vision, saw Atlantean people, how they look – very tall and very slim.

The proportion between the woman and the unicorn are about the same proportion I saw Thunder Paw – she is his size and the horse is the size of a normal horse.

Scientists have found bones of very big people all over the World.

Who is Chak Mol?

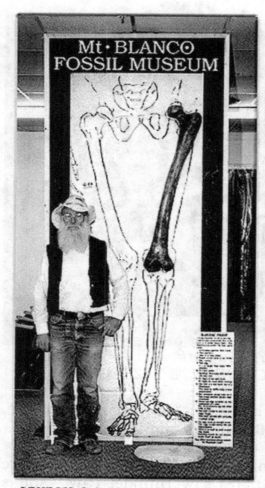

47 inch Human Femur

In the late 1950s, during road construction in south-east Turkey in the Euphrates Valley, many tombs containing the remains of Giants were uncovered. At two sites the leg bones were measured to be about 120 cms "47.24 inches". Joe Taylor, Director of the Mt. BLANCO FOSSIL MUSEUM in Crosbyton, Texas, was commissioned to sculpt this anatomically correct, and to scale, human femur. This "Giant" stood some 14-16 feet tall, and had 20-22 inch long feet. His or Her finger tips, with arms to their sides, would be about 6 feet above the ground. The Biblical record, in Deuteronomy 3:11 states that the Iron Bed of Og, King of Bashan was 9 cubits by 4 cubits or approximately 14 feet long by 6 feet wide!

GENESIS 6:4 ————
There were Nephilim (Giants) in the earth in those days; and also after that when the sons of God (Angels?) came in unto the daughters of men, and they bare children to them, the same became mighty men which were of old, men of renown.

More Info & Replicas available at mtblanco1@aol.com or www.mtblanco.com
Mt. Blanco Fossil Museum • P.O. Box 559, Crosbyton, TX 79322 • 1-800-367-7454

Huge human bones at the Mt. Blanco Fossil museum

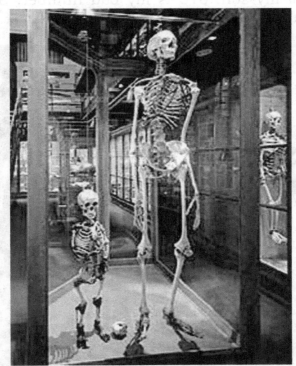

Huge human bones at the London museum of Natural History

Below, I describe what came to me in my visions and dreams regarding Thunder Paw – Chak Mol.

For many years, we had a happy life in Chichen Itza with many rituals and celebrations. In my vision and dreams, I saw lots of joy. Di Cherry told me that during past life regressions, the most emotional, difficult parts of the life come out, so everybody cries during her reading....
I have a feeling that I was a Priest sometimes from the beginning of 800 BC, and happy times went on up to 850 BC – this is my lucky number – and maybe around 870 BC, the drought came and the problems started.

Who is Chak Mol?

Thunder Paw, who is Chak Mol, left and I was grieving because of my son. 870 is my bad number. So maybe this is the year when I died.

Julia and her close friend, Chak Mol, in front of the hotel in Chichen Itza

It was a very emotional day when Thunder Paw left us. It was a farewell day with all kinds of rituals and long discussions.... We never saw him again. He never returned....

I remember how we sat with him the last time at sunset near the water well ("senote") on the big flat rocks, looking to the water. It was our favorite spot. We often sat there and talked. In those days I had an enormous, sad, heavy feeling....

We had droughts for a long time already. It was impossibly hard to collect food for Thunder Paw – he was so big – there was never enough food for him. People brought what they could to him on his platform but there wasn't enough. Yet, most important we, the leaders, couldn't do anything about weather like we did before – the climate conditions had changed dramatically. Thunder Paw had no more success than we did in bringing rain to the countryside. I am not sure, but in this situation, as I understand it, he needed a big crystal for this and he wished to bring this crystal to the top of our big pyramid to make the two as one. I remember I had a dream about it. For those devices to work, he needed clouds to make rain, but there were no clouds for months. It made him sad. People still believed that he could do this, to make rain, but he couldn't.

He left with a few warriors to the faraway temple where we hoped there were no droughts and where there would be food for him.

Later, I think people decided that he went to the sky and started calling him the GOD of Rain.

Because he had an unusually shaped nose compared with the local people, long and turned up at the end, with a bump at eye-level, people began to consider such a feature as the "trademark", the symbol of the GOD of RAIN. According to the hypnosis sessions, he also had blue eyes, white curly hair, long strong chin and straight forehead. I remember that in my dream I always called him: Father. People around me also called him Father, perhaps because he was our noble leader and a teacher. People adored and loved him. I remember feeling this deep emptiness in my heart for a very long time after he left. It was impossibly hard, he was always near me for many, many years, maybe generations, I guess longer than my whole life. I remember sitting in his huge empty house on the way to the sauna and talking to him in my meditation.

It was time when I experience powerlessness. It was a feeling of having reached a dead end. I could not do ANYTHING to change the dry weather to help my people. It was a time when we, nobles, saw and experienced the first breach in people's trust in our Great power. It was a time when *Drought* dictated our lives – not *Man*.

I had a dream, which reminded me of one of the days when we sat with Chak Mol near the water well (senote). I seem to remember that at the time, the senote was full of pure water – filled to the rim – without green algae so that I could see his reflection in the water. I make the name for this dream ZARATUSTRA, but really, I don't have any idea who it was....

Dream # 3
Zarathustra in Water, September 6, 1993

It was a dream at night, but it was like a vision. I have a feeling that I was not sleeping. I was standing on the shore of a little round lake, near a high bluff. I was looking at the reflection in the water. The surface

36

reflected a person of huge size. His reflection was on the surface, but it partially went under water, it was three-dimensional, and I could see him. I was conversing before that about astrology, or just contemplating. I wanted to see him. He was either high in the clouds or standing up on the hill. I thought that, in fact, he was in the clouds, but in order to make it seem real, he offered a conventional way, as if he was standing on the top of the hill and was reflected in the water, in order to calm my imagination down. *I knew that I could not; I was unable to look straight at him. But he wanted to show himself to me – at least as a reflection in the water.*

Leonard Mex Euan, Archeologist at Chichen Itza, and Julia

Diaz Montes Jose Enrique,
Member of the Archeological Society at Chichen Itza

Zoroaster (Latinized from Greek variants) or Zarathushtra (from Avestan Zaraθuštra), also referred to as Zartosht (Persian: زرتشت), was an ancient Iranian prophet and religious poet. The hymns attributed to him, the Gathas, are at the liturgical core of Zoroastrianism.

Zurvanism is a now-extinct branch of Zoroastrianism that had the divinity Zurvan as its First Principle (primordial creator deity). Zurvanism is also known as Zurvanite Zoroastrianism.

In Zurvanism, Zurvan is the hypostasis of Time (and Space). The name, as it appears in Middle Persian, derives from Avestan zruvan-, 'time', with the same range of meaning as in the English language. The name "Zurvan", like 'time', also appears in other belief systems, but in those religions are only nominally related to the Zurvan of Zurvanism.

Although a few recent depictions of Zoroaster show the prophet performing some deed of legend, in general the portrayals merely present him in white vestments (which are also worn by present-day Zoroastrian priests).
He often is seen holding a <u>baresman</u> (Avestan, <u>MP</u> barsom), which is generally considered to be another symbol of priesthood, or with a book in hand, which may be interpreted to be the <u>Avesta</u>.

FACTS

The current name Chacmool is derived from the name "Chaacmol" which Augustus Le Plongeon *gave to a sculpture he and his wife* Alice Dixon *Le Plongeon* excavated *from within the Temple of the Eagles and Jaguars at* Chiche'n Itza' *in1875. He translated "Chaacmol" from Yucatecan Maya as the "paw swift like thunder" (Le Plongeon 1896:157 – Wikipedia, the free encyclopedia).*

Why did people call him "Paw swift like thunder"?

According to my PLR (Past Life Regression) sessions and dreams, people called him "Paw swift like thunder", maybe because the Chak Mol statue is the statue of an Atlantean – a man from Atlantis.

People from Atlantis were very tall like many other ancient, giant human races.
"Most all ancient civilizations believed in the Titans, the race of giant humans that inhabited Earth long ago. Different races knew them by different names. These 7 to 12 foot humanoids were thought to be legendary until the excavation of over a dozen skeletons 8 to 12 feet tall, around the world, shocked archaeologists. The Spanish Conquistadors left diaries of wild blond-haired, blue eyed 8 to 12 foot high men running around in the Andes during the conquest of the Incas" (Wikipedia, the free encyclopedia).

Giants on the USA territory:

1. Large bones in stone graves in Williamson County and White County, Tennessee. Discovered in the early 1800s, the average stature of these giants was 7 feet tall.

2. Giant skeletons found in the mid-1800s in New York State near Rutland and Rodman.

3. In 1833, soldiers digging at Lompock Rancho, California, discovered a male skeleton 12 feet tall. The skeleton was surrounded by caved shells, stone axes, and other artifacts. The skeleton had double rows of upper and lower teeth. Unfortunately, this body was secretly buried because the local Indians became upset about the remains.

4. A giant skull and vertebrae found in Wisconsin and Kansas City.

5. A giant found off the California Coast on Santa Rosa Island in the 1800s was distinguished by its double rows of teeth.

6. A 9-foot, 8-inch skeleton was excavated from a mount near Brewersville, Indiana, in 1879.

7. Skeletons of "enormous dimensions" were found in mounds near Zanesville, Ohio, and Warren, Minnesota, in the 1880s.

8. In Clearwater Minnesota, the skeletons of seven giants were found in mounds. These had receding foreheads and complete double dentition.

9. At LeCrescent, Minnesota, mounds were found to contain giant bones. Five miles north, near Dresbach, the bones of people over 8 feet tall were found.

10. In 1888 seven skeletons ranging from 7 to 8 feet tall were discovered.

11. Near Toledo, Ohio, 20 skeletons were discovered with jaws and teeth "twice as large as those of present day people." The account also noted that odd hieroglyphics were found with the bodies.

12. Miners in Lovelock Cave, California, discovered a very tall, red-haired mummy in 1911. This mummy eventually went to a fraternal lodge where it was used for "initiation purposes."

13. In 1931, skeletons from 8.5 to 10 feet long were found in the Humboldt lakebed in California.

14. In 1932, Ellis Wright found human tracks in the gypsum rock at White Sands, New Mexico. His discovery was later backed up by Fred Arthur, Supervisor of the Lincoln National Park and others who reported that each footprint was 22 inches long and from 8 to 10 inches wide. They were certain the prints were human in origin due to the outline of the perfect prints coupled with a readily apparent instep.

15. During World War II, author Ivan T. Sanderson tells of how his crew was bulldozing through sedimentary rock when it stumbled upon what appeared to be a graveyard. In it were crania that measured from 22 to 24 inches from base to crown nearly three times as large as an adult human skull. Had the creatures to which these skulls belonged been properly proportioned, they undoubtedly would have been at least 12 feet tall or taller.

16. In 1947 a local newspaper reported the discovery of nine-foot-tall skeletons by amateur archeologists working in Death Valley.

17. The archeologists involved also claimed to have found what appeared to be the bones of tigers and dinosaurs with the human remains.

18. The Catalina Islands, off California, are the home of dwarf mammoth bones that were once roasted in ancient fire pits. These were roasted and eaten by human-like creatures who were giants with double rows of teeth.

19. One of the latest accounts of a race of giants that occupied Europe comes from the Middle Ages and involves a surprising figure: Saint Christopher. While modern stories of St. Christopher simply make him out as an ordinary man, or perhaps a somewhat homely man, those who actually saw him had a different story. According to his peers, he was a giant, belonging to a tribe of dog-headed, cannibalistic giants. Jacques de Voragine in The Golden Legend, wrote of St. Christopher: "He was of

gigantic stature, had a terrifying mien, was twelve coudees tall." (A coudee is an antique measurement equal to or larger than the English linear measurement of a foot. According to this ancient account, St. Christopher stood from 12 to 18 feet tall (a fact that has become hidden in or even erased from church history). While Western icons don't picture St. Christopher as contemporary accounts described him, those of the Eastern churches do. Often the suggestion is seen in historic accounts that St. Christopher was the product of a tryst between a human being and an Anubis (a demon-like creature based on the Greek Anoubis, which came from the Egyptians jackal-headed god who was believed to lead the dead to judgment).

In other words, according to the contemporary accounts of his day, St. Christopher was the product of a spiritual being that mated with a human woman. And once again the result of this union was a creature that matched the descriptions of the Nephilim. GENESIS 6:4

There were GIANTS on Earth in those days; and after that, when the SONS OF GOD (Fallen Angels) came in unto the daughters of men, and they bare children to them, the same became mighty men, which were of old, men of renown.
Giants and Ancient History Hidden Proofs Of A Giant Race.
http://www.stevequayle.com/Giants/N.Am/hidden.pro ofs.giant.race.html

Giants in Peru

An excerpt from "The Discovery and Conquest of Peru", Translated with an Introduction by J. M. Cohen, Penguin Books, based on original documents dated 1556. http://www.stangrist.com/giantsdisc.htm

Who is Chak Mol?

Page 33...
5. The seams of pitch at the Cape Santa Elena, the giants that lived there. Near Cape Santa Elena, according to the Indian inhabitants, there once lived giants so great that they were four times the height of an average man. They do not say where they came from, but that they lived on the same food as themselves, especially fish, for...

Page 34...
...they were great fishermen. They fished from balsa rafts, each from his own; for though these rafts can carry three horses, they could take no more than one of these giants. They could wade into the sea to the depth of two and a half fathoms; and they greatly enjoyed catching shark or *bufoes* or other large fish, because these gave them more to eat. Each one of them ate more than thirty men today, and they went naked owing to the difficulty of making themselves clothes.

The Spaniards saw two huge statues of these giants at Puerto Viejo, one male and one female, and an Indian tradition, passed from father to son, tells a great deal about them, in particular the story of their end. They say that a youth shining like the sun descended from the sky and fought against them, throwing flames of fire that pierced the rocks which they struck with holes that are still to be seen. And so the giants retreated to a valley, where they were all finally killed. These Indian tales about the giants were never entirely believed however, until Captain Juan de Olmos of Trujillo, lieutenant to the Governor of Puerto Viejo in the year 1543, who had heard them, commanded some men to dig in that valley. Here they found ribs and other bones so huge that, had it not been for the heads that lay beside them, no one would have believed that they were human. But with this confirmation and in view of the

44

marks of thunderbolts in the rocks, the Indian tradition was accepted as true; and some of the teeth found there, each have three fingers wide and four fingers long, were sent to different parts of Peru. These tokens have convinced the Spaniards that, since this people was much given to unnatural vice, divine justice removed them from the earth, sending an angel for that purpose, as at Sodom and other places.

Giants near Mexico

It has been over 10 years now since Patrick Quirk and I traveled with another 10 more people the back roads of Aztlan searching out the Ancient Halls of Record. We come across nearly 150 mummies and skeletal remains as we searching out the possible locations according the old Spanish Manuscripts that told the tale of the Ancient ancestors of the Azteca. The archaeological specimens shown here were found in the Southwestern portion of the United States bordering the Western Rocky Mountains.

Spiral, conical tombs was found. It feels that this is Hybrid Annunaki offspring. Some 14 feet when standing. Female 8 and 9 feet. The big lady was buried along with some rather unusual metal objects, they were not terrestrial in origin. Symbols and script tell of a sophisticated civilization. Perhaps the survivors of great cataclysms children of Sun and Moon.

There mostly the goddess, the Matriarchal nature of their society, her priest and priestess. They described great devastation, volcanic eruptions, floods. They seem to be telling us about a previous knowledge, in there home land, they include charts, and many examples of mathematics and sacred geometry, from the occult sciences such as there below. So they weren't aboriginals running around eating bugs The carved

45

inscriptions represent ancient astrological and high occult symbols. This type of script is Pre-Egyptian and could date as far as 8,000 BCE. In the Sumerian culture this was the secret language of the priests. These symbols are rare, although we have at 7 or more locations from Central Mexico up the Pacific Coast and well into B.C., Canada

The code, in sacred geometry for Jupiter Square and ancient Sumerian Occult symbol. We have found the writing of 11 different languages in the area from various Euro-Mediterranean which indicate that there was in fact extensive "Global" trade and interaction going on with the people of this area at list 5,000 BCE. Thus this extensive trade and interaction could well have been going on longer than 8,000 years ago.

There was found burial robe made from Camel hair, which had pre-ice age. Examined under an electronic microscope the weave proved so intricate and complex, that the only way we could reproduce it today, would be by computer, using finest silk. Also found sort of netting from Lama hair with technique is that common to proto-Egyptian civilizations in the Mediterranean regions around 3,500 BCE but what is it doing in America?
http://www.robertghostwolf.com/Aztlan/outheretv.htm
ROBERT GHOST WOLF
http://www.lightstreamers.com/ghostwolf.htm

Maybe among them were Chak Mol's relatives?

Because of the location and also because in this amazing website, the author described Atlantis people as "Hybrid Annunaki offspring", because in his opinion Atlantean people are descendants from those who came from space and who were named Annunaki.

So they were part Angels from the cosmos and part humans. You will feel how fragile they felt and being so distant from real people, who are down on Earth, in the book, The Re-birth of an Atlantean Queen – Dream #24, The City Of Crystal Pyramids, June 13, 1993.

Thunder Paw – Chak Mol:

a. He was very big and tall and because of this, he had a very strong voice compared to the small Maya people.
b. He also produced a strong loud sound when he used the crystal device to make electricity – electrical lightning bolt – and as a result, it created thunder and rain in the clouds around him. It looks like because of this sound people called him *Thunder Paw*.
c. The sound of blowing up electricity was often part of his daily routine. This may have affected his capacity to hear and he may have had hearing problems.

Who is Chak Mol?

This photo depicts a copy of the statue of Chak Mol, which was excavated few years ago around the Chichen Itza area. The original of this statue is located now in the Merida City Museum. I was very lucky to find this copy in the Chichen Itza hotel at Piste.

No one knows why, in his statues he is always in the same position, why he lies down and always turns his head to one side.

Chac-Mool is the name given to a type of <u>Pre-Columbian Mesoamerican</u> *stone statue. The Chac-Mool depicts a human figure in a position of reclining with the head up and turned to one side, holding a tray over the stomach (Wikipedia Encyclopedia).*

According to my PLR and dreams, it supports Augustus and Alice Le Plongeon correct translation of his name:

1. Chak Mol – Thunder Paw are one and the same person.

2. Chak Mol was a very tall, real giant person, possibly an Atlantean. I saw Thunder Paw as a very big, maybe a 16- to 18-feet tall man.

3. He needs to lie down each time he talks to people. He also needs to turn his head to one side, because this is the only way he can see people and the expression on their faces. This is the best way to talk and listen to them.

4. He keeps his crystal sometimes up-side down toward his tummy or sometimes he has a disc in his hands. When he activates his device he turns his face to the side, simply trying to protect his eyes.

5. On the bas-relief all around the rim of the Platform of Eagles and Jaguars, all around the top of the temple, a man lies down on his back and turns his head to the opposite side of a long tool he holds in his hands. Possibly, this bas-relief shows how Chak Mol tries to activate rain because I saw him often lie down on this platform: he lies down on his back, points his tool toward the clouds, sending rows of lasers toward the clouds.

Men with goggles
on the bas-relief of the temple of Platform of Eagles and Jaguars

This man has round glasses on his eyes maybe for protection from electrical sparks.[5]

---

[5]   This kind of glasses is found on this ancient carving as well as in another places in Chichen Itza

Who is Chak Mol?

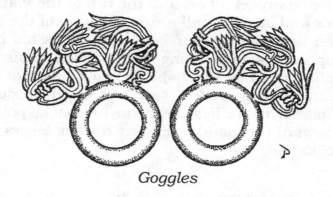

Goggles

("The Origin of the Advanced Maya Civilization in the Yucatan", by Douglas T.)

Chak Mol is obviously wearing goggles

It is possible that wearing a helmet and glasses started to be fashionable to imitate Chak Mol. I heard that

Maya people tried to make special wooden hats for their children so that their foreheads would grow straight – the same as Chak Mol's forehead. Maybe this fashion started and took after the Atlantean, Thunder Paw?

Some people in America managed to open the cranial seam of newborn babies with a piece of wood in order to direct the growth of the brain substance upwards. Depending on the caste, the occipital (the backbone of a skull) of a person was made either flat or elongated. The head of the heir-of-the-throne to the Great Incas was deformed in order to make his features more regular and symmetrical (Religious therapeutic rituals and their role in shaping sotsiotipa; Andrew G. Safronov, safronov@3s.kharkov.ua).

6. Chak Mol – Thunder Paw was a leader and a great teacher. According to the Indian spiritual beliefs, "Nagval" is the name for a teacher who always lies down. Because NAGVAL also means "of the other side of our world", which means a person who can see during their sleep and in their dreams, TONAL is a world, which we always can see.

7. So maybe the ancient Maya decided that the big teacher, Chak Mol, should be shown in the sculptures always in a lying-down position. He is very big, so he was posing in a lying-down position – the only way to see him close-up for those who sculpted the statues.

'Fossilized Irish Giant' (12 feet 2 inches tall) at Broad Street goods station, London, late 19th century. Notice, that the giant is leaning up against a railroad car.

Fossilized Irish Giant (12 feet 2 inches)
Found in London in the 19th Century

Is Chak Mol an ancient, powerful warrior prince?

The name, he said, was given by the ancient Maya to a powerful warrior prince who had once ruled Chiche'n Itza', and was represented by the sculpture (Wikipedia Encyclopedia).

I agree.
Yes, according to my PLR he was a Prince, because his mother was a Queen of Atlantis.

His real name is Thunder Paw. Why did they call him: "powerful", because he was powerful. He was simply big and had much more power than the ordinary person. Mentally, he was also powerful as an Atlantean who brought his special knowledge to the Maya people. It looks like he came from some island, which was originally part of Atlantis.
The statue of Chak Mol is a statue of an Atlantean. He was named "Paw swift like thunder" because he was very tall, big and had a very strong voice compared to the small Mayan people.

How many and how far away are each statue of Chak Mol located?

Twelve chacmools have been located at the Toltec city of Tula, fourteen at Maya Cheche'n Itza', one without provenance is stylistically Aztec, and two are from the Aztec Templo Mayor in Mexico City. Other chacmools have been found at the archaeological site of Cempoala, in the states of Michoacan and Tlaxcala, and at the Maya site of Quirigua' in Guatemala.

If Chak Mol was just a normal human, he would have lived for a maximum of 100 years. How come all other people who lived so far away in different places and maybe hundreds of years apart knew about him, adored him and made his statue?

He was an Atlantean, who lived up to 800 years and maybe much longer. He may have lived in Chichen Itza for a few hundred years and traveled to other places and continued to live there for the rest of his life.

Chac-Mool should not be confused with Chaac

Chac-Mool should not be confused with Chaac, *one of the leading deities in* Maya mythology *associated primarily with the phenomena of rain and thunder, and with whom they are not associated (Wikipedia Encyclopedia). As well as: Chak was the Mayan God of thunder, lightning, rain, and crops.*

I do not agree with this. YES, they are associated. No doubt.

According to the encyclopedia, my PLR, my dreams, the statues of Chak Mol, many drawings and the bas-relief depicting Chaak, the God of Rain, all over the Chichen Itza site:

1. The ChacMool name came from Chaacmol. The name of the GOD of rain is Chaak.
2. At first, people called him ChacMool or Chak Mol – Thunder Paw and considered him as a normal human, except that he was as tall as an Atlantean who knew how to operate crystals, to create loud sounds, electric lightning bolts and to create thunder with the clouds.
3. For this reason, people made him the GOD of RAIN and continued to call him CHAAK.
4. If you look at the profile you can obviously see the European features of the man's face. This face also reminds me of a kind of noble Texas man's profile – with a strong chin. The mask of the God of Rain,

CHAAK, looks exactly like the face I saw – that of Thunder Paw and Chak Mol.

Each corner of Nunnery Complex building in Chichen Itza decorated with the masks of the God Chaak, God of Rain.

Chak Mol with European face (Tulum, Riviera Maya)

Who is Chak Mol?

I was walking in Amsterdam near some souvenir shops when, suddenly, I stopped – literally frozen on the spot! I saw a boy from my own book! He had exactly the same face as the one I saw in one of my hypnosis sessions when Chak Mol was playing with the Maya boys in the ball court. He was a very tall and very slim man – a Nordic type of man, with blond hair and this characteristic profile. The artist who was doing some of the cover designs for me, tried three times to reproduce this face but he just could not replicate what I had seen – the facial features and proportions of the Atlantean man, compared to the normal Maya people, did not match.... I even sent him a photo from the museum where the skeletons of giants beside normal-size people are displayed – to no avail. I tried to find a real person, like this boy or some image on the internet... but nothing.... it still looked like a cartoon – not real. Finally, I gave up.

Back to the real boy; his name is Henk. He was wearing a T-shirt with my luckiest numbers (5 and 8) on it! When I began talking to him, I was even more surprised. I told him that these were my lucky numbers, and he replied that it was the same for him, but that number 7 and 13 were also very special numbers for him! (Do you remember the most important Maya numbers?) Next, I said something that brought me another amazing reply. "Your face looks like a baby face!" I said.

He smiled and replied, "I wish you were my mother! Please, be my mother!" (Remember? I was the mother of Chak Mol, Thunder Paw in Atlantis!)

Henk from Amsterdam

Now look at his profile! His nose has a little bump on the top, it lifts slightly at the end and it's a little long! And his chin and straight forehead are the same as those of Chak Mol! Amazing! Henk's features are exactly the same as those of Chak Mol and those of his father in Atlantis! His profile is also identical to the one carved on the bas-relief in Chichen Itza. He also looks exactly like the God of Rain! On top of this, I call him "boy" here, but he was actually 34 years old. However, he looked way too young for his age – that's how Chak Mol looked. On the photo (below) you can see that he had a real baby face!

Who is Chak Mol?

Henk's "baby face"

We liked each other from the first moment we met. He probably had different ideas, but for me it was the feeling that I had met the real Chak Mol that was important. I was planning to come back the next day to take some photos of his profile for the book, but I was late returning from the trip and when I went to the souvenir shop he had already left, and the next morning I flew back to Canada. So, I apologize for the quality of the profile photo – it's not that great – but you got the idea!

Well…, his looks, his youthful appearance, his numbers and his instant wish to call me "mother" made me think that maybe he was the real Chak Mol, Thunder Paw, an Atlantean man, a long time ago, in another past life. Moreover, he lives in Amsterdam, the city of crystals, diamonds, and diamond factories… Maybe Atlanteans come from Amsterdam, or some of them came to live in this part of Europe after Atlantis sank. Roads and palaces, deep in the ocean, exist near Portugal, not far from the coastline.

If I met him again, I would ask him to go to a past life regression specialist. Maybe he would go, maybe not. For me, as you remember, it was a struggle when my friend mentioned it the first time.

When I was in Chichen Itza during the Equinox, I met a Mexican man who had curly hair and blue eyes like this boy from Amsterdam. He showed me a photo of his two daughters who had white-blond hair and blue eyes! Wow, maybe Chak Mol is the ancestor of many Maya people who live today in the Chichen Itza area?

A Maya man with blue eyes

Where did Chak Mol – Thunder Paw live in Chichen Itza?

In my hypnosis session, I saw him in his big, spacious home in the area near the steam bath, which is located near the "Thousand Columns". I remember it was a tall, high, columned house, which supported a large Maya-style roof. There was a high entrance and maybe it was the only building in the whole of Chichen Itza city where he could go through the door. When I was in Chichen Itza, I only saw one place that would have been suitable, which the guide called the "market", but had no roof – only big columns. I think this was his home, which later, after he left, was used as a meeting place, for meditation or maybe became a market at one point.

The Marketplace and consists of a long, stepped platform giving access to an enclosed, square patio with a central depression surrounded by tall, thin columns (supposedly the highest Mayan columns anywhere). The title *Marketplace* is purely hypothetical.

http://www.geocities.com/atlantis01mx/yucatan_north/chichen_itza.htm

The "Market" or what I feel was Chak Mol's home in
Chichen Itza
photo by Scunner
http://www.panoramio.com/photo/13601513

Where did Chak Mol – Thunder Paw play in Chichen Itza?

During the hypnosis sessions and in my dream I saw him playing with the warriors in the ball court. There was a ring on a wall located 8 meters from the ground, which would have been extremely high for the Maya people to reach, but just perfect for Thunder Paw.

He always wore an outfit similar to what our warriors wore – (except that he had some big shiny jewelry made of some white and silver metal around his neck and I think the bracelet or maybe the ring on his finger were made of the same metal. I am sure about the jewelry around his neck, because it reflected the sun when I looked at him during one of my hypnosis sessions.)

It is known, that the ball was supposed to be driven into the rings, situated on the side panels of the stadium. Although the probability of the four kilogram ball coming into a ring situated at eight meters height seems doubtful. ("Ancient America: flight in time and prostransive. Mezoamerika" Excerpts from the book by GG Ershovoy. Un-copyrighted@Sam, 2003-2006.)

The Ball Court (Juego de Pelota) From the Pyramid of Kukulcan, head north-east to the Great Ball Court, the largest of its kind in the Maya world. There are eight other much smaller ball courts at Chichen Itza and more in other Maya cities, but this one was deliberately built on a much grander scale than any others. The length of the playing field here is 40 feet (135m) and two 25 feet (8 m) high walls run alongside the field. Imagine, then, the significance of this giant court, where the goals are 20 feet (66m) high and the court is longer than a football pitch (Wikipedia Encyclopedia).

61

Who is Chak Mol?

Chal Mol was very tall, but at the same time extremely thin, skinny, light. Maybe the big steps on the pyramid were made for him to climb to the top.

Ring in the ball court

Group of people near the ring
The Great Ball Court itself is the largest not only in Mexico but in all of Mesoamerica.

Maybe, in his honor, they continued to play this game and gave presents to him during the drought season. After Chak Mol left Chichen Itza – out of desperation – the people offered in sacrifice the best person among them – the one who won the game. His Spirit would be sent to Chak Mol, the God of Rain to ask for rain.

(This part was hard for me to type, even now – it has been months since I had my past life sessions. I found out it was my own son that had been sacrificed on that particular day. It was a very hard feeling. I remember the event very clearly. I am seeing his face right now – my tall boy with curly, black hair, dark blue eyes and a fancy tattoo on his high cheekbone.)

How can it be possible that Atlanteans lived in Mexico before?

Retrieved from:
http://en.wikipedia.org/wiki/Gene_Matlock

More than 25,000 books, plus countless other articles have been written about a fabled confederation of city-states known as Atlantis. If it really did exist, where was it located? Does anyone have valid evidence of its existence, artifacts and other remnants? According to historian, archaeologist, educator and linguist Gene D. Matlock, both questions can easily be answered: Only Mexico is named Atlan; Itlan; Otlan; Tlan; Tollan, etc. No other nation on earth can make that claim. Since this is the case and every nation on earth is what it is, Atlantis is Atlantis!

He might be quite convinced that ancient cities from the Mexican gulf to Tenochtitlan are related to some Atl'epec, Tolan, A-tolan and other TLAN like cities.

Who is Chak Mol?

Quote: "Should we continue our fun guessing games about Atlantis for another few millenniums? Or should we confidently begin our search for the submerged half of Atlantis from Atl'epec's (Mexico's) southeast coast? Will the ruins that we'll surely find be those of the real Atlantis?" He believes we should be conducting the search for Atlantis in the Yucatan region of Mexico. Matlock cites place names as one of the compelling proofs.

He also cites an ancient, spiral-shaped harbor with high banks or dikes lining the channels that once existed near San Lorenzo Tenochtitl' Mexico. This layout is very much like that described by Plato for Atlantis's great port city.

****

Sources

1. (Le Plongeon 1896:157 – Wikipedia, the free encyclopedia).

2. Giants and Ancient History, Hidden Proofs Of A Giant Race, http://www.light1998.c om/GIANTS/giants-m.htm http://www.stevequayle.com/index.html

3. An excerpt from... The Discovery and Conquest of Peru, Translated with an Introduction by J. M. Cohen, Penguin Books, based on original documents dated 1556 http://www.stangrist.com/giantsdisc.htm

4. http://www.robertghostwolf.com/Aztlan/outheret v.htm *ROBERT GHOST WOLF,* http://www.lightstreamers.com/ghostwolf.htm

5. Religious therapeutic rituals and their role in shaping sotsiotipa; Andrew G. Safronov, safronov@3s.kharkov.ua

6. "Ancient America: flight in time and prostransive. Mezoamerika" (Excerpts from the book by GG Ershovoy. Un-copyrighted@Sam, 2003-2006.)

7. http://en.wikipedia.org/wiki/Gene_Matlock

8. http://www.geocities.com/atlantis01mx/yucatan _north/chichen_itza.htm

Where to order the book or CDs:

For any information, please visit the website:
http://www.ameliareborn.com/
www.ameliareborn.com

Or contact me at:

contact@ameliareborn.com

YOU TUBE
amelia reborn
2012MayaPriest

To buy this or any of Julia SvadiHatra's five books on line, please visit Amazon.com, BarnesandNobles.com, Borders.com or ChapterIndigo.com and write the title of your choice in the "search window".

CD – available for purchase at www.ameliareborn.com
1. Reading Chak Mol, part #1
2. Reading Chak Mol, part #2

Acknowledgements

Thanks to Mr. Jorge Esma Bazan, Director of Patronato Culture, State of Yucatan, Mexico and to his great team for their effort in keeping the architectural complex of Chichen Itza and other historical monuments in Yucatan in excellent, perfect condition. Their highly organized planning and the maintenance of international levels of standards provide the tourists with the wonderful opportunity to enjoy such important events as the "Equinox in Chichen Itza".

Grateful thanks to Wilma Herrada Dodero, who navigated me with good advices, help and support while I was in Yucatan, Mexico.

To dear Alfons Ven who taught me to ask myself: "Who am I?" His genius gave me the unique possibility to return my self and others to our own selves by using his "miracle pills", changing our lives forever. It helped me in opening the doors to a waterfall of my own enormous amount of energy and in staying in great, dynamic health, optimistic and happy.

Special, deeply felt thanks to the wise, Diana Cherry, who, over the last 60 years, has helped thousands of people getting rid of the heavy burden of their past and find out *who* they really were through studying their Spirit Journey and seeing their lives under a new light.

Special thanks to Roxane Christ, my editor, who encouraged and supported me during the writing of this book. With her thorough knowledge of the language, she helped me, and many other authors, bring our books to life and make them available to readers. She put her full attention and kind heart into my book, and it was a great pleasure working with her.

I express special thanks to my ex-husband, Tim Sviridov. I shall acknowledge the massive efforts of laboriously collecting and systematizing the dreams, which are used in this book, as well as for the production of the beautiful covers.

Who is Chak Mol?

Thanks to Carlos Castaneda for the invention of new terminology, which helped me, and many other authors all over the world, to describe the Spirit world. Going through his books, his message became perfectly clear. I guess because of my past life experience as an ancient Maya Priest, I could read between the sentences what was impossible for him to describe or put into words.

Thanks to the wonderful Crystalinks Metaphysical and Science website which provided with great image sources and information about Ancient Civilizations and helped me with my research.

Special thanks to brave Amelia Earhart who flew the World and became a legend. This enormous effort and her achievements were made available to me in a full and detailed account of her life. It helped me in comparing my life, the life of an Ancient Maya Priest with her life and proved that the Spirit of each person on Earth has many lives. I am deeply grateful for the gift she passed onto me, as a newborn person, who now carries the same Spirit: her experience and knowledge in biology, medicine, art, writing, and drawing, which she acquired and developed during her lifetime. I am thankful for her enormous strength and love for life and adventure. All of this priceless Spirit development is deeply appreciated by all other re-born people in these Spirits and those who will be reborn in future and continue to carry Spirit light through the chain of lives.

Thanks to the Ancient Maya Priest who gave me wisdom, knowledge about the other side of life: energy, auras, how to connect with Spirits, Gods and Goddesses. All of which were passed onto me in the form of an amazing friendship with plants, animals and echoing rocks; understanding their tender souls. I am also grateful to him for passing onto me his enormous strength, love and care for his people. He helped them survive through terrible droughts in Mexico and he was strong enough to sacrifice his own son for their wellbeing.

To my lifelong friend and companion in my dreams, the Holy Spirit, my Guide who lives somewhere in the Universe, on the Other Side and for giving me support, helping me travel in my dreams through the planet and our Universe. He is the one who was talking to me throughout the years, teaching me and educating me in my dreams and helping me connect with other Spirits, Gods and Goddesses. I give you prayerful thanks.

To some amazing High Power and to my extended family on the Other Side, who are my Guardian Angels, who care about me, and who help me navigate in this life to avoid danger, make the right decisions and warn me ahead of time by talking to me daily through the numbers' code, I give thanks.

Special thanks to GOD who blessed me and saved my life, and as a result, enabling me to write this book.

Read More...

In the book, **"THE PRIEST"** you will find details of Julia's SPIRIT JOURNEY from her life as an Ancient Mayan Priest of Chichen Itza. 2000 years old secrets revealed: how he performed ceremonies and rituals on top of the pyramid, the Spirit world, sacrifices, symbols and the life of the ancient Maya people in Chichen Itza – a Message from them to the present-day civilization passed on to us. Meeting with God and angels, contacts with ancient Goddesses, Persian Goddesses, new Atharvan images, Zarathustra, ghosts, visiting a real Buddhist temple ... are all in Ancient Priest of Chichen Itza reincarnated by Julia SvadiHatra.

In the book, **"KUKULCAN"** an Ancient Maya Priest comes to you through thousands of years and giving rare knowledge what you can expect after your own death. All people will live in Spirit world between lives. The spirit world is full of amazing colors, lights, dynamics speed and magic things which do not exist in our world. Travel in Time? Teleportation? Meeting with Kukulcan-Quetzalcoatl. Who is he? From where GIANTS come on Earth? Why people build pyramids? Do we live in the Past or in the Future?

In the book, **"AMELIA REBORN?"** Amelia is talking to us. Astonishing secrets are revealed. Was Amelia meant to die according to some "secret plan"? Through the author's past life experience, Amelia is able to describe the last minutes before her death, how she enters Heaven. Why was she lost? Why is it impossibly difficult to find her? Is it a curse by ancient Egyptian or Mexican spirits on those who are "playing games" around Amelia's disappearance?

What is common between Amelia and the Ancient Priest of Chichen Itza?

In this book you will also find details of Amelia's SPIRIT JOURNEY from her life in Ancient Egypt. Did Amelia belong to a royal family of Ancient Egypt or was she a Priestess there? A unique Egypt's ancient initiation ceremony of a Goddess, meeting with Egyptian Goddesses and magic of the Holy Spirit of Bast, the Royal Cat Goddess, intriguing Anubis, communication with an Ancient Priest & Pharaoh, swimming in the efir oils, present to the Great Cheops pyramid, ancient ritual inside the tomb, talking to mummies, GIANT Pharaohs... are all in this truly Mysterious Magic Egypt.

In the book, **"THE REBIRTH OF AN ATLANTEAN QUEEN"** you will find the complete story about the Spirit Journey of Amelia and all her other past lives as a Priest of Chichen Itza, an Atlantean Queen, Ancient Egyptian royal Priestess, Julia Svadihatra and even one future life. This big book contains all 4 books we just mentioned: Priest, Who is Chak Mol, Amelia Reborn, Kukulcan and an additional chapter: The Rebirth of an Atlantean Queen about life in Atlantis. Was Amelia an Atlantean Queen in her past life? Did she carry with her secrets of the crystal pyramid and how to re-ignite its energy? In this book Amelia's Spirit went back to her past life in Atlantis and her abilities began to emerge in this life time in a new re-born person!

Enjoy reading.

Exclusive editor of all 5 books:
Roxane Christ, www.1steditor.biz